STOCKING STUMPERS

KIDS RIDDLES

By S. Claus

RED-LETTER PRESS, INC.
Saddle River, New Jersey

Red-Letter Press, Inc.
P.O. Box 393, Saddle River, NJ 07458
www.Red-LetterPress.com
info@Red-LetterPress.com

ACKNOWLEDGMENTS
SANTA'S SUBORDINATE CLAUSES

Compiled By:
Jack Kreismer

Editor:
Jeff Kreismer

Cover & Page Design:
Cliff Behum

Special Mention:
Sparky Anderson Kreismer

STOCKING
STUMPERS

KIDS RIDDLES

FOWL PLAY

1.

How does a comedian like his eggs?

2.

What do you get if you cross
a chicken with a cow?

3.

Why did the chicken cross
the basketball court?

4.

What's a hen's favorite vegetable?

5.

Why did the turkey cross the road?

Seasonal Stumper

What do Santa's beard and a
Christmas tree have in common?

They both need trimming.

ANSWERS

1.

Funny side up

2.

Roost beef

3.

It heard the referee calling fowls.

4.

Eggplant

5.

To prove he wasn't chicken

Seasonal Stumper

How can you tell if a tree is female?

Look for its skirt.

QUACKERS

1.

How come ducks don't fly upside down?

2.

Why wouldn't anyone go
to the duck doctor?

3.

What's yellow, plastic,
and holds up banks?

4.

What do you get if you cross
a duck with an alligator?

5.

What's a duck's favorite snack?

Seasonal Stumper

What runs all around Santa's
reindeer pen without moving?

A fence

ANSWERS

1.

Because they might quack up.

2.

Because he was a quack.

3.

A robber duckie

4.

A quack-odile

5.

Quacker-Jacks

Seasonal Stumper

Where does mistletoe go to become famous?

Holly-wood

SCHOOL SILLIES

1.

How do musicians prepare for tests?

2.

What three letters can be
found in your blood?

3.

What do smart students eat
their hamburgers on?

4.

Why did the 50-watt bulb
flunk out of school?

5.

At what school do you
learn to greet people?

Seasonal Stumper

Where do polar bears vote?

The North Poll

ANSWERS

1.

By studying their notes

2.

D, N, A

3.

Honor rolls

4.

Because it wasn't very bright.

5.

"Hi" school

Seasonal Stumper

What do you get when you cross
Santa Claus with a flying saucer?

A U-F-HO-HO-HO!

CROSSOVERS

1.
Why did the chicken cross
the playground?

2.
Why did the hen only go
halfway across the road?

3.
Why did the chewing
gum cross the road?

4.
Why did the duck cross the road?

5.
Why didn't the chicken cross the road?

Seasonal Stumper

How come the elf pushed his bed into the fireplace?

He wanted to sleep like a log.

ANSWERS

1.

To get to the other slide.

2.

She wanted to lay it on the line.

3.

Because it got stuck to
the chicken's foot.

4.

It was the chicken's day off.

5.

Because it heard there was a Kentucky
Fried Chicken on the other side.

Seasonal Stumper

What did Rudolph say to Mrs. Claus?

Nothing- deer can't talk.

From Sea to Shining Sea

1.

What happens when you throw a green rock into the Red Sea?

2.

Where does a mermaid sleep?

3.

What lies at the bottom of the sea and shakes?

4.

What does a shark like to eat with peanut butter sandwiches?

5.

What did Cinderella wear when she went swimming in the ocean?

Seasonal Stumper

What's an ape's favorite Christmas carol?

Jungle Bells

ANSWERS

1.

It gets wet.

2.

On a water bed

3.

A nervous wreck

4.

Jellyfish

5.

Glass flippers

Seasonal Stumper

How many presents can Santa put into his empty sack?

Just one, because then it's not empty anymore.

SPORTS SHORTS

1.

What kind of basketball nets
do they use in Hawaii?

2.

Who was the fastest man in the world?

3.

How come you can't get a straight
answer from wrestlers?

4.

What do heavyweight fighters
wear under their clothes?

5.

What's a rubber band's favorite
part of a baseball game?

Seasonal Stumper

What do you give a mummy for Christmas?

Wrapping paper

ANSWERS

1.

Hula hoops

2.

Adam- He was first in the human race.

3.

They're hard to pin down.

4.

Boxer shorts

5.

The seventh inning stretch

Seasonal Stumper

How do you fire Santa Claus?

Give him the sack.

HORSING AROUND

1.
What story is told by a small horse?

2.
Where do you take a sick pony?

3.
What do you call a pony with laryngitis?

4.
Why did the racehorse hide behind a tree?

5.
How is a leaky faucet like a race horse?

Seasonal Stumper

Can Santa jump as high as a 20-foot chimney?

Sure – Chimneys can't jump.

ANSWERS

1.

A pony tale

2.

To the horse-pital

3.

A little hoarse

4.

To change his jockeys

5.

They're both off and running.

Seasonal Stumper

What is Santa's nationality?

North Polish

PUN-ISHMENT

1.

What do you call an alligator in a vest?

2.

Why did the spider turn
on his computer?

3.

Why did the turtle cross the road?

4.

Why couldn't they play
cards on Noah's ark?

5.

How come teddy bears
are never hungry?

Seasonal Stumper

What do you call Santa's helpers?

Subordinate clauses

ANSWERS

1.

An investigator

2.

To go to his web site

3.

To get to the Shell station

4.

Because the elephant sat on the deck

5.

They're always stuffed.

Seasonal Stumper

How do sheep in Mexico say "Merry Christmas"?

"Fleece Navidad!"

MILKING IT

1.
Why does a milking stool
only have three legs?

2.
What animal does
Russian milk come from?

3.
What do you call a cow
that's given birth?

4.
What do you call a cow with no legs?

5.
What do you get from pampered cows?

Seasonal Stumper

What do you call a giraffe at the North Pole?

ANSWERS

1.

Because the cow has the udder

2.

Moscow

3.

De-calf-inated

4.

Ground beef

5.

Spoiled milk

Seasonal Stumper

Why can't Santa's elves play pro basketball?

They don't measure up.

CRIME TIME

1.

Where do they put criminals that steal Hershey's chocolate?

2.

What did the judge say when the librarian broke the law?

3.

Why was the detective at the beach?

4.

Why did the cop go to the baseball game?

5.

What kind of person steals soap?

Seasonal Stumper

What's black and white and red all over?

Santa Claus coming down the chimney

ANSWERS

1.

Behind candy bars

2.

"I'm going to throw the book at you."

3.

There was a crime wave.

4.

Because he heard
someone had stolen a base

5.

A dirty crook

Seasonal Stumper

Why does Scrooge love Rudolph?

Because every buck is dear to him

GRRR-OANERS

1. What dog loves to take baths?

2. What do you call a dog that's left-handed?

3. Why aren't dogs good dancers?

4. What do you get when you cross a cocker spaniel, a poodle, and a rooster?

5. What did the dog say when it sat on sandpaper?

Seasonal Stumper

Which one of Santa's helpers was a vegetable rock star?

Elfis Parsley

ANSWERS

1.

A shampoodle

2.

A south paw

3.

Because they have two left feet

4.

A cockerpoodledoo

5.

"Ruff!"

Seasonal Stumper

What's red and white and falls down a chimney?

Santa Klutz

FOOD FOR THOUGHT

1. Why did the salad make the chef turn around?

2. How do you make a hot dog stand?

3. What's fat, green, and goes "Oink, oink"?

4. What cereal goes "Snap, Crackle, Squeak"?

5. How do lions like their meat cooked?

Seasonal Stumper

What is Santa's favorite Easter candy?

Jolly Beans

ANSWERS

1.

She didn't want him to see her dressing.

2.

Play the national anthem.

3.

Porky Pickle

4.

Mice Krispies

5.

Medium roar

Seasonal Stumper

How come Santa keeps bells on his bathroom scale?

Because he likes to jingle all the weigh.

IT'S ABOUT TIME

1.

What happens when you
make a clock mad?

2.

What time did the duck wake up?

3.

What do you call a grandfather clock?

4.

What does a clock do when it
hasn't had enough to eat?

5.

Why did the man put his
watch under the desk?

Seasonal Stumper

What falls around Christmas but never gets hurt?

snow

ANSWERS

1.

It gets ticked off.

2.

At the quack of dawn

3.

An old timer

4.

It goes back for seconds.

5.

He wanted to work over time.

Seasonal Stumper

What comes around the holidays, is bright
and festive and swims in the ocean?

A Christmas cod

ANIMAL ACTS

1. What do you call a dead parrot?

2. Where did the skunk sit in church?

3. What do you call someone who steals from kangaroos?

4. What do you call a pig's laundry?

5. What do you get if you cross a pig, a sheep, and a fir tree?

Seasonal Stumper

What goes, "Ho, Ho, Ho, Swish"?

Santa Claus making a jump shot

ANSWERS

1.

A polygon

2.

In its own pew

3.

A pickpocket

4.

Hogwash

5.

A pork-ewe-pine

Seasonal Stumper

What does Santa Claus become on Christmas Day?

A "beat-nick"

CRACKING YOLKS

1. What happens when an egg laughs hysterically?

2. What do you call a scrambled egg wearing a cowboy hat?

3. What do you get when you cross a hen with a cement truck?

4. What is Santa's favorite drink?

5. What do you get if a hen lays an egg on top of a barn?

Seasonal Stumper

What kind of Christmas candles burn longer?

None- They all burn shorter.

ANSWERS

1.

It cracks up.

2.

A Western omelet

3.

A bricklayer

4.

Eggnog

5.

An eggroll

Seasonal Stumper

What is Santa's favorite state in the U.S.?

Idaho! Ho! Ho!

CAT TALES

1.

What's a cat's favorite dessert?

2.

What do you call a cat with
eight legs that likes to swim?

3.

What is a cat's favorite song?

4.

What kind of cats like to go bowling?

5.

What do you call a cat
that eats lemons?

Seasonal Stumper

What's red and white and full of holes?

Swiss Kringle

ANSWERS

1.

Mice cream

2.

An octopuss

3.

Three Blind Mice

4.

Alley cats

5.

A sourpuss

Seasonal Stumper

What kind of bug hates Christmas?

A humbug

ALPHABET SOUP

1.

What begins with T, ends with
T, and is filled with tea?

2.

Which letters are not in the alphabet?

3.

What has three
letters and starts with gas?

4.

What is a pirate's favorite letter?

5.

What's the longest English word?

Seasonal Stumper

When does Christmas come before Thanksgiving?

In the dictionary

ANSWERS

1.

A teapot

2.

The ones in the mail

3.

A car

4.

ARRRRRR!

5.

Smiles- It has a mile between the s's.

Seasonal Stumper

What do you get when you deep-fry Santa Claus?

Krisp Kringle

What's Up, Doc?

1.

Why did the doctor get mad?

2.

Why did the mattress go to the doctor?

3.

What doctor operates on fish?

4.

Why did the fireplace call the doctor?

5.

Why did the banana go to the doctor?

Seasonal Stumper

What goes, "Ho, Ho, Ho, Plop"?

Santa laughing his head off

ANSWERS

1.

Because he didn't have any patients

2.

It had spring fever.

3.

A sturgeon

4.

Because its chimney had the flu

5.

Because it wasn't peeling well

Seasonal Stumper

What do you call people who are afraid of Santa?

Claus-trophobic

SNOW FOOLIN'

1.

What do you get when you cross
a snowman with a vampire?

2.

What did one snowman
say to the other?

3.

What did the cop say when he
saw the snowman stealing?

4.

What do you call an old snowman?

5.

What do snowmen eat for breakfast?

Seasonal Stumper

What's Santa's favorite sandwich?

Peanut butter and jolly

ANSWERS

1.

Frostbite

2.

"Do you smell carrots?"

3.

"Freeze!"

4.

Water

5.

Frosted Flakes

Seasonal Stumper

How do you know when Santa's in the room?

You can sense his presents.

Ho! Ho! Hodgepodge

1. Why was the computer exhausted when it got home from work?

2. Why didn't the skeleton go to the dance?

3. Why did the fish swim in salt water?

4. When is a door not a door?

5. What do you call a country full of pink automobiles?

Seasonal Stumper

What goes "Baaaa! Humbug!"?

Ebenezer Sheep

ANSWERS

1.

Because it had a hard drive

2.

He had no body to dance with.

3.

Because pepper made him sneeze

4.

When it's ajar

5.

A pink carnation

Seasonal Stumper

What did Mrs. Claus say to Santa when she looked up at the sky?

"Looks like rain, dear."

WHAT DO YOU CALL…?

1.

What do you call a sick bird?

2.

What do you call a fake noodle?

3.

What do you call a duck that gets straight A's in school?

4.

What do you call a dog that does magic tricks?

5.

What do you call a sleeping bull?

Seasonal Stumper

What do Santa, Mrs. Claus and the elves put in their salad at the North Pole?

Iceberg lettuce

ANSWERS

1.

An ill eagle

2.

An impasta

3.

A wise quacker

4.

A labracadabrador

5.

A bulldozer

Seasonal Stumper

What do you call Santa when he stops moving?

Santa pause

CHEESY JOKES

1.

How come Swiss cheese is the pope's favorite kind of cheese?

2.

What cheese do people live in?

3.

What did the cheese say before having its picture taken?

4.

How do you get a mouse to smile?

5.

What do you call cheese that isn't yours?

Seasonal Stumper

What do sheep say to shepherds at Christmas?

"Season's Bleatings!"

ANSWERS

1.

Because it's hole-y

2.

Cottage cheese

3.

"People."

4.

Say, "Cheese."

5.

Nacho cheese

Seasonal Stumper

What kind of laundry detergent do
Santa and Mrs. Claus use?

Yule Tide

GETTING THE BUGS OUT

1.

What do you call a
rabbit with insects all over it?

2.

What kind of fly has a
frog in its throat?

3.

Why was the insect
looking for a garbage can?

4.

What do fireflies eat?

5.

Where's the best place to buy bugs?

Seasonal Stumper

Why did Rudolph go to the orthodontist?

Because he had buck teeth.

ANSWERS

1.
Bugs Bunny

2.
A hoarse fly

3.
Because it was a litterbug

4.
Light snacks

5.
At the flea market

Seasonal Stumper

What do you get when you cross Santa with a dog?

Santa Paws

ELEPHANTS ARE IN THE ROOM

1.

What is large, grey, and
wears glass slippers?

2.

What do you get if you cross
an elephant with a fish?

3.

What do you get if you cross an
elephant with a kangaroo?

4.

Why aren't elephants
allowed on the beach?

5.

Why are elephants so poor?

Seasonal Stumper

Who delivers Christmas gifts to shellfish?

Lobster Claus

ANSWERS

1.

Cinderelephant

2.

Swimming trunks

3.

Great big holes all over Australia

4.

They can't keep their trunks up.

5.

Because they work for peanuts

Seasonal Stumper

What is the cleanest reindeer called?

Comet

PIECE OF CAKE

1.

Why are candles put on top
of a birthday cake?

2.

Why did the cake go to the doctor?

3.

Why did the cupcake go to the doctor?

4.

What do they serve at
birthday parties in heaven?

5.

What is a ghost's favorite kind of cake?

Seasonal Stumper

What do you get if you cross an
iPad with a Christmas tree?

A pineapple

ANSWERS

1.

Because it's too hard to put them on the bottom.

2.

Because it was feeling crumby.

3.

It had frostbite.

4.

Angel food cake

5.

"I scream" cake

Seasonal Stumper

Who says, "Oh, oh, oh!"?

Santa Claus walking backwards

FOR THE BIRDS

1.

Why do sea gulls live by the sea?

2.

Why do hummingbirds hum?

3.

What's a wise bird's favorite subject?

4.

What do you get if you cross
a parrot with a shark?

5.

What brand of soap do birds use?

Seasonal Stumper

What do you call an elf who steals gift wrap
from the rich and gives it to the poor?

Ribbon Hood

ANSWERS

1.

Because if they lived by the bay, they'd be bagels.

2.

Because they can't remember the words.

3.

Owlgebra

4.

A bird that will talk your ear off

5.

Dove

Seasonal Stumper

Why are Christmas trees such bad knitters?

They're always dropping their needles.

PIGGING OUT

1.

Who's the smartest pig in the world?

2.

What do you call a pig that's a thief?

3.

Why should you
never tell a pig a secret?

4.

What do you call a pig
that's lost its voice?

5.

What do you call a pig with no legs?

Seasonal Stumper

Why did the thief run off with Santa's sack of presents?

*He figured they were
grab bag gifts.*

ANSWERS

1.

Albert Einswine

2.

A hamburglar

3.

They love to squeal.

4.

Disgruntled

5.

A groundhog

Seasonal Stumper

What is red and white, red and white, red and white?

Santa rolling down a hill!

Ho! Ho! Hodgepodge

1.

What did everyone call Old MacDonald when he joined the army?

2.

Why did the girl get stung when she put on her coat?

3.

What's a boxer's favorite drink?

4.

Why was the kangaroo asked to be on the basketball team?

5.

What do you get if you throw Daffy Duck into the Pacific Ocean?

Seasonal Stumper

What is a Christmas tree's favorite candy?

Ornamints

ANSWERS

1.

GI, GI, Joe

2.

It was a yellow jacket.

3.

Punch

4.

Because it was good at jump shots.

5.

Salt water Daffy

Seasonal Stumper

What do you get if you cross Santa with a detective?

Santa clues

ALL EARS

1. What do you call a gorilla with a banana in both of his ears?

2. How much does it cost for a pirate to get his ears pierced?

3. What has ears but cannot hear?

4. What do you call a bear without an ear?

5. What do you give to a fisherman who's going deaf?

Seasonal Stumper

Which one of Santa's reindeer is the fastest?

Dasher

ANSWERS

1.

Anything you want- He can't hear you.

2.

A bucc-an-eer

3.

A cornfield

4.

B!

5.

A herring aid

Seasonal Stumper

What did Rudolph say before telling a joke?

"This will sleigh you."

BAA-D JOKES

1.

What did the polite sheep say
after holding the barn door open?

2.

Where do sheep get haircuts?

3.

What actor is a favorite of sheep?

4.

What make of car do
sheep like the most?

5.

What do you get if you cross
a sheep with a porcupine?

Seasonal Stumper

What did the dog breeder get when she crossed
an Irish Setter with a Pointer at Christmastime?

A pointsetter

ANSWERS

1.

"After ewe."

2.

At the baa-baa shop

3.

Christian Bale of Hay

4.

Lamb-orghini

5.

An animal that knits its own sweaters

Seasonal Stumper

Why is Santa so good at karate?

He has a black belt.

Auto-motives

1.
Where do automobiles
do the backstroke?

2.
When is a car not a car?

3.
Why did the driver put a
rabbit in his gas tank?

4.
What's worse than
raining cats and dogs?

5.
What do you call someone who
draws pictures of motor vehicles?

ANSWERS

1.

In car pools

2.

When it turns into a driveway

3.

Because he needed the
car for short hops.

4.

Hailing taxis

5.

A car-toonist

Seasonal Stumper

What song do skunks sing at Christmas?

Jingle Smells

READ ALL ABOUT IT!

1.

Where does a librarian sleep?

2.

What does a book do when it's cold?

3.

What did the frog say when
he landed on a book?

4.

What do you call a book
that's about the brain?

5.

What did one library book
say to the other?

Seasonal Stumper

What does a 500-pound partridge in a pear tree
need more than anything else at Christmastime?

A new pear tree

ANSWERS

1.

Between the covers

2.

It puts on a book jacket.

3.

"Reddit, reddit, reddit."

4.

A mind reader

5.

"Can I take you out?"

Seasonal Stumper

What does a cat on the beach have
in common with Christmas?

Sandy Claws

BATTER UP!

1.

What do you get when you cross
a baseball pitcher with a carpet?

2.

How is a baseball team
similar to a pancake?

3.

Why are frogs good outfielders?

4.

What do catchers wear on Halloween?

5.

Why did the baseball player
decide to shut down his website?

Seasonal Stumper

What did the big grape say to the
little grape on Christmas?

"'Tis the season to be jelly."

ANSWERS

1.

A throw rug

2.

They both need a good batter.

3.

They never miss a fly.

4.

Face masks

5.

Because he wasn't getting any hits.

Seasonal Stumper

If athletes get athlete's foot, what do astronauts get?

Missile toe

WHAT DO YOU GET...?

1.
What do you get when you cross a million dollars with bank employees?

2.
What do you get when you cross a praying mantis with a termite?

3.
What do you get when you cross a dog with a cat?

4.
What do you get when you cross a chicken with a cow?

5.
What do you get when you cross a large Japanese city with a child's stringed toy?

Seasonal Stumper

What does Scrooge wear to play ice hockey?

Cheap skates

ANSWERS

1.

Fortune tellers

2.

An insect that says "grace"
before eating your house

3.

An animal that chases itself

4.

Roost beef

5.

Tokyo-yo

Seasonal Stumper

Where do the Three Wise Men go
to get their robes tailored?

Bethle-hem

WHAT DO YOU CALL...?

1.

What do you call a grandmother duck?

2.

What do you call two
spiders that just got married?

3.

What do you call a
frozen police officer?

4.

What do you call a frog with two legs?

5.

What do you call a flying rabbit?

Seasonal Stumper

Where does a frog kiss at Christmastime?

Under the mistletoad

ANSWERS

1.
Graham Quacker

2.
Newlywebs

3.
A copsicle

4.
Unhoppy

5.
A hare-plane

Seasonal Stumper

What do you use to decorate a canoe for Christmas?

Oar-naments

WHAT'S WHAT?

1.

   What drink do you give
   to a sick crocodile?

2.

   What happens when you
   light a duck's tail?

3.

   What kind of fish is good at Old Maid?

4.

   What does the sky do when it's filthy?

5.

   What's black and yellow and
   goes zzub, zzub, zzub, zzub?

Seasonal Stumper

How do the reindeer start a race?

Santa says, "Ready, Set ... Doe!"

ANSWERS

1.

Gator-aid

2.

It becomes a firequacker.

3.

A card shark

4.

It showers.

5.

A bee flying backwards

Seasonal Stumper

Why was the desktop computer
so quiet on Christmas Eve?

Because not a creature was
stirring, not even a mouse.

WHY, OH WHY?

1.

Why isn't the man in the
moon married?

2.

Why couldn't the skeleton
pay attention in school?

3.

Why did Mickey Mouse
travel into outer space?

4.

Why do skiers like to hear about
blizzards on the weather report?

5.

Why did the car need a wig?

Seasonal Stumper

What kind of music do the elves play
in the North Pole workshop?

Wrap music

ANSWERS

1.

What woman would marry a man who stayed out all night?

2.

Because his mind was somewhere else

3.

To find Pluto

4.

Because snow news is good news

5.

Because it had bald tires

Seasonal Stumper

Why does Santa spend so much time in the garden?

Because he likes to hoe, hoe, hoe

WHERE IN THE WORLD?

1.

Where do hornets go
when they get sick?

2.

Where do smart dogs never shop?

3.

Where do you weigh a whale?

4.

Where do rabbits go
after they get married?

5.

Where did the young cow eat lunch?

Seasonal Stumper

What did Adam say on December 24th?

"It's Christmas, Eve."

ANSWERS

1.
To the waspital

2.
At flea markets

3.
At the whale-weigh station

4.
On a bunnymoon

5.
In the calf-eteria

Seasonal Stumper

Which Christmas carol never gets sung?

The Second Noel

IT'S AS EASY AS ABC

1.

How do you spell a
mousetrap in three letters?

2.

What starts with "p" and ends with
"e" and has thousands of letters in it?

3.

What are a banker's favorite vowels?

4.

What two letters
describe freezing weather?

5.

Which two letters of the
alphabet mean you look nice?

Seasonal Stumper

What's the difference between a
Christmas alphabet and the regular alphabet?

The Christmas alphabet has No-el.

ANSWERS

1.

C-A-T

2.

Post office

3.

I-O-U

4.

I-C

5.

Q-T

Seasonal Stumper

Why does Santa go down the chimney on Christmas Eve?

Because it soots him

IT'S A NUMBERS GAME

1.

What did 0 say to 8?

2.

Why didn't the two 4s want dinner?

3.

Why was the number 6 so frightened?

4.

How do you make 7 even?

5.

Why can't your nose be 12 inches long?

Seasonal Stumper

What's a librarian's favorite Christmas song?

Silent Night

ANSWERS

1.

"Nice belt."

2.

Because they already 8

3.

Because 7 8 (ate) 9

4.

Take away the "s."

5.

Because then it would be a foot

Seasonal Stumper

What's red and green and guides Santa's sleigh?

Rudolph the red-nosed pickle

AROUND THE WORLD

1. Where do lambs go for their vacation?

2. What's in the middle of Paris?

3. What did Tennessee?

4. Where is the English Channel?

5. What do you call someone from Detroit who talks too much?

Seasonal Stumper

How do the reindeer keep in shape for their Christmas Eve journey?

Ice-ometrics

ANSWERS

1.

To the Baa-hamas

2.

The letter "r"

3.

The same thing Arkansas

4.

That depends on your cable TV provider.

5.

A Motor City Mouth

Seasonal Stumper

What did Santa's helper do when he wanted to improve his toy making skills?

He read an elf-help book.

SHOW BIZ STUMPERS

1.

Why couldn't the kid watch
the pirate movie?

2.

Why couldn't Dorothy tell the
bad witch from the good one?

3.

How popular was the
movie about the hot dog?

4.

What do you call an overweight E.T.?

5.

Why don't fish watch TV?

Seasonal Stumper

What kind of pictures do Santa's helpers take?

Elves

ANSWERS

1.

It was rated ARRRR.

2.

Because she didn't know
which witch was which.

3.

It was an Oscar wiener.

4.

Extra Cholesterol

5.

They don't want to get hooked on it.

Seasonal Stumper

Why do people call Santa Claus Saint Nick?

Because he's really bad at shaving

HOT POTATOES

1. What do you get when you cross an elephant with a potato?

2. What do you call a potato after it's been sliced?

3. What do you call a baby potato?

4. What do you call a lazy baby kangaroo?

5. What do you call a potato at a football game?

Seasonal Stumper

What Christmas song do dogs like?

Bark, The Herald Angels Sing

ANSWERS

1.

Mashed potatoes

2.

Chip

3.

Small fry

4.

A pouch potato

5.

A spec-tater

Seasonal Stumper

Why wouldn't the kid eat broken candy canes?

He didn't want them unless
they were in mint condition.

GINORMOUS

1.

What goes, "MUF OF IF EEF"?

2.

What do you get when you
cross a doorbell with a giant?

3.

Why is the Jolly Green
Giant such a good gardener?

4.

How do you talk to a giant?

5.

What's a giant's favorite food?

Seasonal Stumper

What is red and white and goes up
and down and up and down?

Santa Claus stuck in an elevator

ANSWERS

1.

A giant walking backwards

2.

Ding Dong King Kong

3.

He has two green thumbs.

4.

Use big words.

5.

Squash

Seasonal Stumper

What do the reindeer take for an upset stomach?

Elk-a-seltzer